F*ck you, Cancer

...and the cell you rode in on

Humorously Toxic

By Ritch Gaiti

Also published under the title "Welcome to Cancerland" for those who prefer a less toxic title ☺

Fuck you, Cancer

And the cell you rode in on

Humorously Toxic

Published by:

www.SedonaEditions.com
ISBN: 9781731492784

For Jan,
Keep Juggling

and

For Dawn,
The Bravest Person I know

1
Sharks in the Basement

I had never given much thought to the nature of my demise, should that ever occur. However, if I had conjured up a list of usual suspects of my eventual incapacitation and passing, cancer still would not have made the line-up. It would not have even been considered for consideration.

However, *if* it had appeared on my list as one of my potential executioners d' jour, it would have been in the quest of completeness, not because I considered it within the realm of possibility. And, certainly it would have fallen to the very bottom, right after *being eaten by sharks in my basement.*

> *Potential ways that I could, you know, die:*
> *96. Taking a shower with two or more supermodels*
> *97. Eating a pomegranate*
> *98. Falling off of my bedroom slippers while playing an opera on my banjo*
> *99. Being eaten by sharks in my basement*
> *100. Cancer*

To be clear, to the best of my knowledge, I have never had sharks or any other predatory fish in my basement, except for Attila, my kosher goldfish. Moreover, I live over forty miles from the ocean and there is no conduit waterway that a shark could take to get to my house — and if it did, it is unlikely that it could open the basement door. The prevailing logic notwithstanding, I opted for shark-proofing my house as part of the termite guarantee.

To summarize; in my mind, I had a slightly greater chance of being attacked by sharks in my basement than getting cancer.

I was wrong.

2

It's a splotch, right?

Doc P, my Pulmonologist, studied the computer screen. This could not be a good sign. Of course, just having a Pulmonologist is not a good sign. If I had a list of *Things I don't want to have*, Pulmonologist would be near the top, way ahead of Periodontist and a notch behind Criminal Lawyer. Of course, I wouldn't want to have to have a Parole Officer, a Bankruptcy Attorney or Shingles either.

I watched the Doc. Any second now; he would turn to me, straight faced and say, "My bad, must have been a splotch on the X-ray machine."

"No cancer?" I would query rhetorically to stretch the moment of victory.

"Cancer, schmancer. It was a mere splotch on the machine. It'll be ok after a few treatments of Windex. Heh." he would joke apologetically.

I would nod; slowly turn to Virginia who, by now, would be weeping in relief. She, of course, was prepared to weep with any news. Without the slightest sign of *I told you so*, I would gallantly wipe her nose on my sleeve. I, less given to panic, would stand smugly silent, knowing that it was a mere splotch, which is only fatal to X-ray machines.

What's taking so long?

"It's a splotch, right?" I uttered louder than I intended.

Doc P studiously hovered over the computer screen, which reminded me that I had left a game of Spider Solitaire unfinished on my laptop, once again falling short of a new record of two consecutive wins.

The Doc slowly turned, glanced at me, then at Virginia and back to me again — a triple glance-over — another sign of impending bad news. Virginia's beautifully manicured nails dug into her skin, which began to match the hue of her new coral, polish. Suddenly, the walls of my invulnerability softened to the consistency of slightly overcooked Wheatena. I avoided looking at Virginia, as she may not have picked up the same sign of imminent doom. After all, it was my job to protect her from unnecessary peril, real or imagined.

"System's a tad slow today." Doc P. offered, "get the results in a jiff." He lip-smiled, avoiding exposing his teeth which would have indicated jocularity or wittiness, clearly inappropriate for the occasion.

I returned his lip-smile, accompanied by the appropriate nod of acknowledgement, momentarily secure in the knowledge that my immortality remained intact. My Wheatena hardened.

Cancer happened to other people, not me. After all, I did not work in a coalmine or with radioactive asbestos or have genetic history or bask in the sunshine with a reflector or chain smoke. Ok, I did smoke but I quit cold turkey almost thirty-five years ago. Cancer was other people's disease — it never entered my psyche, much less my body.

Allow me to back up a tad. I didn't just happen upon Doc P because I was ultra-health conscious.

It started with a small cough. When I say small, I mean the postnasal drip, annoying-but-not-worth-mentioning-cough, except that it probably saved my life. Now, I owe everything to that cough, which I have since named Ed Feldman and keep in a small cardboard shoebox under my bed.

I undoubtedly would not have seen my regular Doc except for my wife's strong recommendation, seconded by my mother, followed by my daughter and my sister and the lady at the dry cleaner. With flaming torches in hand, or maybe they were *flaming torch* iPhones apps, they marched under my window, chanting: "See the doctor, see the doctor."

I saw Doc H. because they were right and my cough had overstayed.

"Sounds like pneumonia." My regular Doc observed.

"Pneumonia? I never had pneumonia, are you sure?"

"Nope. Take an X-ray." She added.

An X-ray? I hate extra steps in any process. Another little thing to add, then delete, from my to-do list. I spent most of my life knocking things off of my to-do list in my quest for the fabled empty nothing-to-do list. Alas, it would not be today.

So, as the Doc prescribed, I:

1) Took it easy,

2) Took antibiotics,

3) Took an X-ray, and

4) Took another X-ray a couple of weeks later.

The cough persisted.

The Doc called me before our follow-up appointment. Let me be clear, the *Doc* called *me*. Usually, Docs have their receptionist call to remind me of the appointments that they have already reminded me of with a little card, a follow-up email, a text, an evite and a voice mail. But, if the Doc wanted to save a few bucks and call herself, that's ok with me. With a tad of concern and urgency in her voice, she added a to-do to my list:

5) A Catscan.

Not being driven to unnecessary anxiety or consternation, I took the Catscan without much thought, certain that whatever she was looking for was somewhere else.

"You don't have pneumonia." The Doc offered.

"Thought so." I humbly replied without some much as tad of *I told you so* in my voice. "Just a little cough right? No biggie. Be gone in a day or two. Right?"

"Do you have a Pulmonologist?" She inquired.

Doc P, my newly found Pulmonologist, turned excitedly from his computer screen. "You are a very lucky guy." He announced.

"Knew it!" I exclaimed. "Just a little cough right? A little Robitussin and take it easy for a few days, right? Plenty of liquids. No biggie, right?"

I jumped up and high-fived the Doc and Virginia and followed up with a surprisingly coordinated wave. Virginia and I morphed into the twist while Doc did the chicken dance. Still attached to the Blood Pressure machine, I triggered a Code Blue throughout the University Medical Center of Princeton.

Ok, that didn't happen.

"Stage I." Doc P. corrected me.

"Huh?"

"See that?" He pointed to a small splotch on my Catscan. "A small adenocarcinoma, near the lining of your right lung, but it has not spread so it is Stage I. You're a lucky guy."

"Yes."

I turned to Virginia who held back a quivering upper lip.

"I'm lucky." I said. "Stage one."

We hovered over the Catscan admiring our little splotch. After all, moments like this should be shared and remembered. Our own little adenocarcinoma.

The little bugger measured 1.7 centimeters, Doc P. reported proudly as he spanked its bottom. I whipped out my metric-to-decimal-to-fraction conversion app on my iPhone and quickly calculated that the little bugger was about two and a half feet wide.

"About the size of a dime." He corrected.

That was the good news: it was Stage I, it had not spread and it was on the very reachable portion of my right lung. It was a maverick cell, a lone wolf, an octopus without tentacles, an isolated culprit, a sole perpetrator, an army of one, a single operative.

That was good news. Stage I Cancer; the best possible news I could hope for except for the *splotch on the X-ray* good news, or *it's just a little cough* good news, or *nothing happened because I wasn't here in the first place because there had been nothing wrong with me* good news.

Unfortunately, through all of the really good news, all I heard was:

"You have cancer."

FUCK!

3

Five Minutes Earlier. .

. . . before the word *carcinoma* was uttered in my presence, sending my life into a new downward spiral, my immortality had been intact. Unjustly suspected and accused of harboring the worst criminal known to mankind, I sat into the exam room secure that I would be fully vindicated, freed, and pardoned from my family's worst fear. I expected full exoneration — and perhaps an apology. Ok, no apology. But I did expect a medical version of a splotch, no biggie, better be safe than sorry.

I fully expected to be declared cancer-free and I probably would have been a tad miffed at having to undergo that whole process that created ripples of anxiety through three generations of my family.

Then it hit — I realized that I had been wrong about my invulnerability. Blindsided by a cold dose of reality, which I have always considered far over-rated.

Four minutes before the Doc told me the news, I realized that I had been living in denial. Not denial of the actuality because there had been no actuality until the Doc uttered it. In spite of my incredibly fortified logic, history, optimism and delusion, I had denied the possibility that I actually *could* have cancer. For the first time, my optimism took a nosedive and I crossed from optimism into pessimism, from hope to gloom, from invulnerability to mortality.

Could it be that I was mortal?

I *knew* it before the Doc said it, which made hearing it even worse. Somewhere deep within my self-assuredness and confidence, even though I knew that I was wrong about not seriously considering cancer as a tenant in my bod, I still counted on the Doc giving me good news and proving that I was wrong about being wrong. I was wrong about that as well.

Denial is resilient.

I put my manface on and tried to pay attention to Doc P.

"Do you have a Thoracic Surgeon?" Doc P asked compassionately with a touch of empathy and kindhearted understanding.

A Thoracic Surgeon?

Two weeks ago, I didn't have a Pulmonologist; or a Catscan; or a two and a half foot carcinoma, whatever that was. I checked my iPhone for Thoracic Surgeons; I had contacts for my mom's Podiatrist and the local pizza places — alas, no Thoracic Surgeons.

4

The Doofus on the Bike

My perspective of immunity had not been based solely on my delusions of my invulnerability. It had been based on a plethora of facts and experience carefully stirred with some sound rationalization. Some background may prove useful.

I was in my sixties in the year of the occurrence. Not a health maven or a workout junkie, I still maintained reasonably good health and reasonable fitness — in spite of a couple of back surgeries and the requisite potpourri of childhood ectomies. Curiously, one of my childhood goals was to achieve a perfect school attendance record, which I was forced to abandon in the third week of the first grade, after I got the measles. Yet, I am very proud of myself for attempting such a lofty feat and coming so close to accomplishing it. Regretfully, I shall never get that chance again.

My dreams dashed, I settled on being the blackboard monitor like the rest of my family. Coming from a long line of blackboard monitors and not one to accept defeat easily, I focused on being the best blackboard monitor I could be.

I look, act and feel like I'm ten years younger than my, until now, healthy years. I attribute my condition to my youthful appearance, a combination of good genes and a reserve of latent immaturity. My dad, who was in great shape, lived to almost ninety, played tennis well into his eighties. Mom, who hustles gin rummy at the local Y, is spirited, independent, active, and alert. I inherited my athletic prowess from her. She looks twenty years younger than her late nineties. Until recently, she rarely went to a doctor or dentist, not counting the Podiatrist whom I think she had a crush on since she was in her seventies and he was not born yet. I inherited most of my genes from her.

I have a clean family history with few instances of cancer. My first cousin Hal passed of cancer a few years ago. Strangely, since he was younger than me, I did not consider it a hereditary threat. Perhaps it was because he lived in Staten Island. Then there was Uncle Hy who passed over thirty years ago at the hand of cancer. But since he was not technically my uncle, just a good family friend who was ceremoniously awarded the Uncle title because of closeness of his relationship, I did not consider this within the scope of my family health history. Aunt Bea was also awarded the Aunt designation. She did not get cancer but I thought that I would mention her.

I miss Hal and Uncle Hy and Aunt Bea, even though she did not get cancer.

Alas, I digress. To be totally transparent and forthcoming, my living and eating habits could come into question. My eating habits hovered around normal, with a slight preponderance towards sweets, particularly in my early years. Basically, I ate what I liked. I wasn't reckless or excessive about eating, except for my addiction to Twizzlers and still enjoy an occasional après-dinner Twizzler. Other than that and my extreme dislike of most cheeses, I ate two to three squares a day plus the occasional late night snack.

I smoked when smoking was actually good for you. It was that special time when smoking made you popular and actually did not cause cancer or make you smell — a beautiful time when friends gathered in droves, filled the room with an acrid and bonding miasma as the less fortunate non-smokers huddled in small masses in the cold outdoors.

When I was fourteen, I looked like I was eleven. I smoked a pipe but only when I rode my bicycle so my parents wouldn't find out. In retrospect, they would have been quite embarrassed — not by the smoking, but by having their oldest offspring, a fourteen year old, eleven-year-old-looking doofus kid, ride around the neighborhood smoking a pipe. Of course, had I realized the doofus-ness of the pipe/bike thing, I would have reconsidered and smoked a Hava-Tampa, the cigar for non-cigar-smoking aficionados.

Initially unable to master the art of inhaling, I took smoking classes from my older cousin, lest I be outcast into the cold with the other loser non-smokers. I practiced regularly while showering and became quite proficient and the first in my crowd to master the art of blowing smoke rings. In fact, I once accomplished the legendary smoke ring within a smoke ring feat but the smaller smoke ring clipped the edge of the larger one invalidating my record achievement.

Then for fifteen irresponsible and blissfully ignorant years, I smoked a pack of cigarettes a day. I migrated among the brands that made me manlier, cool, and immediately accepted in any social situation. Yes, my smoking gave me the confidence to be different just like everyone else. I oscillated between regular and menthol, long and short, filtered and non-filtered.

Then, I quit, cold turkey. No fumar.

As a child, I had an abundance of immaturity, which I strived to preserve until my later years. While most kids recklessly consumed all of their immaturity when they were young, with a final burst expended in college, I had so much that I could spend freely and, with careful planning and foresight, stash enough away for the future. It seemed like a shame to waste such a God-given talent. I basically focused on the now and would let the future take care of itself. To wit, my younger brother, Don, had seven cash register banks that couldn't be opened until each accumulated ten dollars — seven banks, each one securely held $9.90. Conversely, I had one bank with a screwdriver wedged into the drawer to provide immediate access to the errant dime or quarter that may have been left behind during my last raid.

Alas, I deviate.

Given my perpetual immaturity, I could never see myself as an old man: old, perhaps, but still the doofus kid on the bike.

I never considered that I might not become old.

5

Doc T and the Pepperoni

An affable and knowledgeable Thoracic Surgeon, Doc T knew exactly what to do. He considered my general good health and youthful appearance in his evaluation and recommendation for attacking the invasive bastard. I didn't tell him to add ten years to my age because of my young looks, or about my fourteen-year-old pipe/bike thing, or about my near-perfect attendance record at P.S. 222. I figured that was in my medical records.

He described the procedure.

"A lobotomy?" I queried incredulously.

Virginia explained that Doc T said lobectomy not lobotomy — although she did inquire if the Doc could do both.

"Think of it this way," Doc T explained. "The right lung is divided into three sections, called lobes. Each is about the size of a folded up slice of pizza."

He saw the curious look on my face.

"Regular, not Sicilian," he clarified. "It's very hard to fold Sicilian slices."

I nodded; clearly he had been trained well.

"On the top slice, there's a solitary piece of pepperoni."

I stood up. "The carcinoma." I said proudly. I sat.

"Yes. The carcinoma. I want to remove the top slice, er lobe, from your lung, pepperoni and all. Your lung will expand and fill the empty space. You won't miss it."

"And?"

"And?"

"And, what happens after that?" I queried. "Am I clear, done, finished? With you, that is. Nothing personal. Will I be cancer-free?"

He hesitated. "We will monitor you every six months or so for five years. If the cancer has not returned, you stand a very good chance of being cancer-free."

"How good?"

He dimmed the lights and turned on a PowerPoint slide show on his laptop. A screen floated down from the ceiling.

The Doc stood before a massive pie chart that illuminated on the screen.

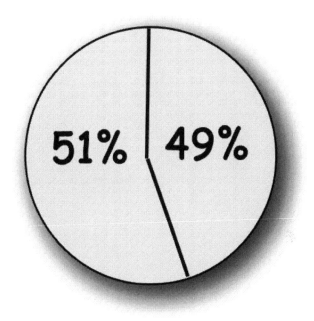

"49%?" I queried.

He turned the lights on as the screen disappeared into the ceiling.

"Forty nine percent of lung cancer patients survive five years."

"I have only a 50/50 chance of surviving?"

"Forty nine."

"Yes."

"Of course, that's the statistics. But you have a lot of things going for you — you are in good health, you are relatively young."

I wondered if I should bring up the bike/pipe thing.

Whatever the odds, they seemed better than not having the surgery. As far as I was concerned, it was just another ectomy. Besides I never used my lungs that much.

"How about next week?" Doc asked.

Facing what could be the most important decision of my life, except for when I removed the training wheels from my tricycle, I considered it carefully. I looked at Virginia and she returned the same. I paced the room, circling Virginia and the Doc. Time was critical. I needed a decision. I paced.

"How about Monday?" Virginia blurted out.

"Recycling day." I informed.

She nodded. I continued pacing.

"Tuesday?" She responded.

Tuesdays always seemed like a lucky day, I was born on a Tuesday and Tuesdays were devoid of municipal activities and national holidays. I turned to the Doc. She was right.

"How about it, Doc. Tuesday?"

So Tuesday it was, one week from today I would be once-again cancer-free, just like I was two weeks ago before my little cough, Ed Feldman.

Of course, we sought and received a second opinion, which differed slightly from Doc T's approach. Doc T2 thought that Doc T, planned on removing too much lung. Instead of removing the whole lobe, he recommended . . .

"A wedge resection."

"Huh?"

"I will remove a small wedge of your lung." Doc T2 explained.

"Not the whole lobe?"

"Not the whole lobe." He said smugly.

"With the pepperoni." I added, proudly displaying my newly acquired medical prowess.

"The pepperoni?"

"The carcinoma." Obviously, not all surgeons went to the same med school.

"Yes."

"Is that better than taking my whole lobe?"

"Definitely. What if, down the road," he continued. "You get cancer in another part of your lung and more has to come out? You will be down one lobe. Nope," he metaphored, "It's like throwing out the spare tire."

"Unless you have run-flat tires." I interjected. "Of course, I would need run-flat lungs, which, I don't believe they have come out with yet."

Virginia threw me a look, which I discerned to mean:

a) *Now is not the appropriate time to be funny, which you are not*, or;

b) *Shut up and let the doctor talk,* or:

c) *Did you feed the dogs before we left?*

I immediately responded with one raised eyebrow, which is our standard look for: '*certainly I fed the dogs. Jeez.*' It's good to be totally in synch with someone. Many couples finish each other's sentences. Being far more advanced in our relationship, Virginia not only finishes my sentences, she oft starts them as well. She will construct my entire sentence and tactfully correct what I would have said, thereby having the entire conversation without my participation. I find that this minimizes marital discord and builds rapport. Of course, it is a great time saver as well.

Alas, I digress.

We digested the second opinion then we called Doc T and chatted a bit about the upside and downside, pros and cons, and pluses and minuses of both approaches to obliterate the diminutive poison pill from my bod.

But which Doc was right?

The Docs had different approaches. However, they did both agree that the little squatter had to be evicted but differed on how much to take with it. Also, they both agreed that the other Doc was a putz and probably went to med school online and should have been a proctologist.

We decided to go with Doc T because he was affable and offered frequent flier miles with every surgery, successful or not. He would take the entire folded-up slice, complete with pepperoni.

I was greenlit for Tuesday, the day of my birth.

Mangia. Ciao, Cancro!

6

I Calculated My Odds of Survival

to Know which

Bills to Pay

I had confidence in Doc T and his robotic scalpel but what happens after that? What is my destiny, my providence, my fortune? Confused, concerned and hungry, I needed answers that I could not get from a doctor — answers from a much higher authority. I made a PB&J sandwich and checked Google.

I sifted through all 14,300,000 Google results whilst stopping only for bio breaks and cookies. The Mayo Clinic explained that, based on statistics, the *survival rate* means cancer patients are still alive five years out. The Mayo Clinic said 49%; Doc said 49%. I was comforted that Doc T read the same Google link that I did. I have a 49% chance of being alive five years from now if a bus or other public conveyance does not hit me.

The National Cancer Institute's website said, 54% survive, a tad more than the Doc's and The Mayo Clinic's stats. Fifty four percent — a much more optimistic projection. Who knows, I may be in that errant 5%. Clearly, the National Cancer Institute had been more progressive and probably marked on a curve. I checked several more websites in search of even further cutting-edge Cancer Institutes, perchance to find the one that has calculated a 68 or 74%, or even the very elusive, 99% survival rate. To my dismay, I found even lower numbers. The more I read, the more I became unsatisfied, depressed and confused. I made another sandwich.

I needed more information. I had to confer with an even higher authority.

"Fifty fifty." Hochman muttered as we mulled over a beer. Actually, I had a glass of red wine and he had a Whiskey Sour. Hochman, my long-time amigo, always offered a curious slant on the goings-on of whatever was happening. Filled with an expansive expertise of just about anything, relevant or not, Hochman had been a valued confidante through the most trying of times. Most of those times, he was the one that made it trying. This time, however, the culprit had been that isolated pepperoni wedge in my chest.

"Actually, forty nine, fifty one." I corrected.

"A mere flip of the coin."

"Only a forty nine percent chance that five years from now that we would be having a beer together." I doodled '49%' on my cocktail napkin, making little eyes out of the % sign.

"Or a Whiskey Sour and a glass of . . ." Hochman stickled the particulars.

"Or, fifty four percent, if you believe the National Cancer Institute." I added to demonstrate my newly acquired expertise.

"Fifty four percent. I like that much more. You're probably in that extra five percent." Hochman always had a way of mashing facts into irrelevancy.

"That would be good."

"Of course, it's not so good if your Doc is right."

"Yeah." I crossed out the 49 and wrote 54 on the napkin. I also added eyebrows to the little eyes.

"Actually, either would be good because the overall survival rate for all stages is closer to fifteen percent." Hochman added.

"Really?" I added a nose and a tiny frown to the % sign.

"Really. And over half the people die within one year of being diagnosed. Half the people." He raised his glass. "Cheers."

"Cheers." I didn't raise my glass to clink, causing Hochman to misjudge the velocity of his clink; a small spillage of Whiskey Sour ensued. "According to you, I may not make it to the check, which, by the way, you are picking up."

"Understood." He licked an overflow of Whiskey Sour from the rim of the glass. "You caught it early. Only fifteen percent catch it early. That's lucky."

"I guess."

"Yes. Fifteen percent — only one out of six and two thirds people, rounding up to the nearest two thirds of a person. You could have been one of the other five and two thirds people or, who knows, you could have been the two thirds of a person. Of course, you would have been shorter. What are the odds?"

"Four to one."

"Huh?" He queried.

"Four to one that if you keep rambling, I will empty the remaining contents of my Pinot Noir in your lap." I resisted sipping my wine thereby ensuring adequate spillage onto his Dockers.

"I see. But the numbers don't lie." He rambled on. "You are likely to drink with me for the next five years and henceforward, ad infinitum, through eternity and beyond."

"Wonderful."

"Of course, it could be worse. If you caught it later, it would be next year or the year after or later so this conversation would not be happening now." He sipped Whiskey Sour through a straw and raised his glass again. My wine had not yet made it to my mouth.

"To the women who harassed you to seeing the Doc." He toasted.

We clinked and Hochman spilled Whiskey Sour over his hand and my doodled cocktail napkin. I watched the '54%' dissolve into oblivion, eyebrows, frown, and all.

Hochman, not known for his persistence, tried once again. He raised his glass.

"To the dry cleaning lady."

"Why are we toasting her? She was included in the last toast." I tried to hold back the words but they had already passed my lips. I should be so lucky with my wine.

"You didn't specifically mention her."

"She was implied. The dry cleaning lady is always implied in all of my toasts." Again, I regretted answering.

"Well, my clink didn't include her. To the dry cleaning lady."

I raised my glass and performed an evasive clink maneuver, narrowly missing his near empty glass. He deked left and reached in for the clink again as I deftly finessed my glass left, then right, avoiding contact once more. Then, in a graceful arc, I brought the glass straight to my mouth thereby ending the possibility of another clink.

Defeated, he squeezed the contents of my napkin into his glass. Eyebrows floated atop the Whiskey Sour.

"You know you aren't cheering me up." I said, reminding him of his mission for the foreseeable future.

"Was I supposed to?"

"It would be nice."

"You will beat the odds and probably live forever."

"Thanks. I feel better now."

I ordered another round and told the waitress to give Hochman the check.

"You worried?" Hochman inquired as he tried to unclog his straw.

"What, me worry?"

"You are worried."

"Not really. Well, maybe a little but only a tad. Not a whole tad, half a tad or less."

"Odds are in your favor, almost."

"Don't know if I'm more concerned about the future or the past."

"Como?"

"I mean, how did I get cancer? Me? Of all the people I know, why me?"

7

I Wrote a Sincere and Heartfelt Note to Communicate My Feelings:

I Didn't Tell Anyone About It

Normally upbeat and not given to unnecessary worry, I approached this whole episode casually, somewhat confident of the outcome. Not because I had any particular insight into the subject or had any fitness or nutritional advantages — but because I've always considered *worry* a highly over-rated cranial activity with dubious benefits. Worry creates stress, which creates anxiety, which begets irrational activity causing unintended outcomes, which creates more worry. In fact, worry is one of the most self-perpetuating reflexes, ranking far ahead of hiccups.

Somehow, I have always felt that whatever crisis life threw at me — puberty, financial, health, mild acne, askew relationships, and the like — I would always come out the other side better than I went in. I was protected. No matter what. That single thought, that notion of ultimate conquest whatever dragon rose from the shithole, kept me going. In fact, it became almost a self-fulfilling prophecy — because I believed that I would prevail, I usually did. However, this time was different.

Before I dealt with quality of life; now, I dealt with life itself. I could ask *why me?* But I know that there are thousands of me's asking why. Is it just the numbers?

Seven percent get lung cancer in their lifetime. One out of fourteen. No pain, no symptoms - maybe I was just due. How did I get it? Certainly I could not think of a rational cause – smoking was out, so was everything else. But something got into my system when I was unaware.

But I had been lucky. If not for Ed Feldman, my pesky cough, some caring and persistent women and a very diligent Doc, I could be in a far different place.

Truthfully, I had been more concerned that the people I cared about were more worried about me than I was about myself. Of course, I couldn't let them see my concern and cause more worry, which would then impact my concern and so forth. I began to worry about my worrying about them worrying about me.

I treated surgery as just another item on my to-do list, a step in the process to get back to where I was. Confident of the outcome, I had approached the operation nonchalantly. Hadn't I conquered all of my prior ectomies with flying colors? Yes, I assured myself. But, surgery is surgery. What if something goes wrong? What if the Doc was not aware of my mortality and somehow blunders and leaves his iPad in my vacated lobe? Rationally, I knew the odds of such occurrences were pretty low because doctors take pretty good care of their IPads.

In my youth, I never worried about dying. In fact, the nature of my death did not occupy as much of my idle thoughts as the most compelling and important of all questions:

Who would attend my funeral?

I had speculated on who might miss my special day so that I may develop the appropriate retaliation plan if they passed before me. To ensure that no one would be overlooked, I kept a mental list of good friends, ex-good friends, potential friends, colleagues, rivals, adversaries, acquaintances, neighbors, local merchants, Facebook/Twitter/Google + friends and followers, relatives in good standing and associates who would just show up to be seen at such a prestigious event. In fairness, I eliminated members of my Cub Scout troop, since I was a member for only one week, and those folks whose funeral I probably would not attend because I would be busy not going to their funeral. I had a quandary that had effectively kept my mind occupied during history or bio class, blackboard monitor practice, corporate town hall meetings, commutes and personnel reviews.

As secure I as I was in the outcome of my imminent surgery, I needed to be prepared.

I wrote a note — the kind that says things that I should probably say out loud but the occasion somehow was never right. I didn't want to create unnecessary concern so I didn't tell anyone about it. I left it on my desk, right between the instructions on how to use the TV remote and the care and feeding of my dogs.

Of course, should the note come into play, only the dog sitter would read it and since I did not mention her in the note, it is unlikely that she would pass it on. In fact, since she knew how to care for my dogs already, it is unlikely that the note would ever be discovered unless someone was perusing my hard drive in my private *'Open in the event of my untimely death by sharks in my basement or other unseemly causes'* folder. For the public, the note will also be available on my refrigerator, website, blog, Facebook, Instagram, Twitter, Google Plus, and as an ebook on Kindle. I am considering posting a reading of the note on YouTube as well and looking into selling the movie rights.

In any case, to date, the note had not been needed but my family can see it for the first time in the Appendix, if they buy the book and read that far. I discourage skipping ahead to the note because it is not that funny and you will certainly lose your place.

I hesitated to give it to my family before my demise, lest I omitted anyone or somehow blew the order of gratitude and placed someone's name after someone else's name like I did in my public school graduation speech after achieving the *P.S. 222 Blackboard Monitor of the Year,* a school-record, three times and the distinction of getting a C+ in every class I had taken. [Author's note: I maintained the straight C+ through college. Just saying.]

A private word about *the note* to my family and friends . . . .

Dear friends and family et al,

If I omitted your name, I will correct it in Note 2.0, which should be released prior to the next time I almost die. If, on the other hand, you are reading this book and the note after my demise, then everything is exactly as I wrote it and there will be no future releases of the Note.

Please contact Customer Service with any support issues.

Thank you,

The Management.

8

The Juggler Conundrum

Just a few weeks before my cough became the watershed of my life, Jan; my brother's bro-in-law (aka my bro-in-law-in-law) discovered a brain tumor. He wasn't fortunate enough to have a small cough to cause the dry cleaning lady to prompt him to see the doc. I thought of him as I readied for my journey. Unbeknownst to me, I would soon be in a similar state but, unlike my stage one slice of pepperoni, his was a stage four Kielbasa.

Brain surgery immediately followed. Two days later, I visited him in the hospital. As I entered his room I eyed a small crowd hunched around his bed. Expecting the worst, I approached the bed cautiously, lest I disturb the solemnity of the moment. As I peered through the engrossed crowd, I spied Jan standing by his bedside juggling three balls. Let me be clear — he was standing and juggling two days after brain surgery. Nary a ball hit the ground.

I forged my way to the front of the crowd to witness this highly unlikely and improbable feat. Just hours following brain surgery, a procedure that could have the direst of all consequences, Jan stood and juggled — a remarkable and implausible occurrence. I marveled at his resilience and attitude — rivaling my own in optimism.

"What's your secret?" I had to ask.

"Secret?" He responded with nary a break in his rhythm.

"You just had brain surgery and now you're juggling. What's your secret?"

"Concentration. Focus on the highest ball. And breathing. Breathing is good."

"Yes. I breathe a lot — almost every day. But I can't even juggle one ball. Well, maybe could do one as long as I don't have to catch it." Feeling somewhat inept, I added. "When I was younger I could smoke a pipe while riding my bike."

Jan smiled as we shared a unique skillset common to brotherhood.

Jeez, a brain tumor, yet he smiled and juggled.

But herein laid the conundrum. Jan was an excellent physical specimen — a runner, a workout-aholic, a disciplined and health-conscious eater. I was very much like him, except in all of the aforementioned traits.

Yet, we both got cancer; discovered quite coincidentally within weeks of one another. Why?

I repeated my new mantra:

Don't feel sorry for yourself schmuck. Besides, you can learn how to juggle if you really want to.

9

The Best Ectomy Ever

A nurse entered and picked up my chart. "Name?"

I answered quickly and deftly. She was not going to get me on that one.

"Very good. What is your birthday?"

Again, after reading *Pre-Op for Dummies*, I had been fully prepared.

She nodded and graded my chart and handed it to me. I quickly looked to see if all the hours of prep had been worth it. And there at the top of my chart, in perfect red-pencil, it stood like it had throughout my school years — a perfect C+. I shall add this to my scrapbook immediately after pre-op, surgery, post-op, ICU and recovery.

"Is this the one that's coming off?" She inquired as she touched my right leg.

"Huh?"

"Gotcha. Just wanted to see if you were paying attention." She smiled and put a red cap on my head.

A second nurse entered, asked my name and birthday and took my vitals. She departed with my vitals.

The first nurse returned and I assured her that I was still me and my birthday had not changed. She said: "Ready for breakfast?"

I nodded and she stuck an IV in my arm. "Enjoy." More hospital humor.

After the entire pre-op preamble, she whisked my red cap off and replaced it with a green one. I was good to go.

Virginia and I held hands for a moment. I considered telling her about my goodbye note but decided that she would be better off if I maintained my cavalier attitude. She had enough worry on her own. Besides, if it came into play, she would find it when she looked for the instructions for the remote. I did, however, remind her that recycling was every two weeks.

The anesthesiologist came into introduce herself and hooked up something to my IV. The next thing that I remembered was nothing.

I did not remember anything after that until two hours after surgery when I awoke in ICU, which was standard for post lung surgery.

Amazingly, I sat up in bed, felt well, coherent, without the excessive pain that I had anticipated. I credit that to an excellent surgeon, his minimally invasive technique, great nurses, competent orderlies and transport, high quality suspension on my gurney, a terrific hospital, a great family, and my new best friend, morphine.

Just one week after I had discovered that I had cancer, I killed the parasitic bastard and now I was cancer-free. The Toxic Avenger was dead. Considering the amplified stakes of this surgery, this was one of my favorite ectomies of all time. Perhaps because I had so many friends and family come to visit. I don't remember anyone except my mother showing up for my tonsillectomy. And she didn't even show for my vasectomy, which, I believe was her form of a passive aggressive protest against my officially ending her flow of grandchildren.

Clearly, the upper lobe of a right lung was far more precious than a tonsil or an appendix or a snip of the vas deferens. In fact, not having the surgery was far more risky than having it. No one ever died from not having a vasectomy.

They marveled at my quick bounce back immediately after the surgery and hardly noticed the missing lobe. Most of all, they marveled at my attitude throughout. I credit that to my aforementioned immaturity and delusional invulnerability, which, as it turns out, may not be so delusional after all. I dodged a bullet, evaded the grim reaper and cheated death. I hit the morphine button twice to celebrate.

Fuck you cancer, and the cell you rode in on.

Hochman popped in to cheer me up. Ordinarily I welcome the diversion of Hochman's warped logic but I felt somewhat uneasy about entertaining while being bed-ridden in a backless gown with tubes exiting from multiple body portals. I would try to hasten his well-intended visit.

"For you," he said, handing me a limp balloon dangling from a string.

"It isn't even blown up." I keenly observed.

"I deflated it. I figured you could use it as exercise on your lungs."

He made sense. I kept that to myself.

I stretched the balloon and read the inscription.

"Happy Bat Mitzvah?"

"They were all out of *Happy Lobectomy* balloons. It was *Happy Angioplasty* or *Congratulations on your*

Liposuction or *Cheer Up! At Least Your Good Friend Stopped Into the Gift Shop Instead of Showing Up Empty-Handed.*"

"Thanks for the balloon. It's the best and most thoughtful *Happy Bat Mitzvah* balloon I have ever received. There's a forty nine percent chance that I shall cherish it forever."

"How goes it?" Somewhat out of character, Hochman asked a serious question. "I mean, how are you feeling?"

"Actually, pretty good. TV, an occasional pop-in friend, present company notwithstanding, good nurses. And I order my meals from a menu whenever I want."

"Nice."

"You want to know the best part?" I didn't wait for a reply as I motioned him to come closer. I whispered: "The catheter."

"The catheter? That's the best part."

"Yep. Don't have to do anything. I just lie here. Whenever I have to go, I just go. Don't have to get up. Don't have to hold it back. No standing, no aiming, no flushing. I just go."

"You just go?" Hochman was dubious.

"Yep. I just go. Anytime. When I'm watching TV, when I'm on the phone. When I'm lying here just chatting about catheters with a friend."

"Now?" Hochman's eyes widen.

"Yep."

"You are going?"

"As we speak."

"Right now?"

"In my catheter." I smiled an extremely satisfying smile.

Hochman said something about leaving his blinkers on.

"Thanks again for the balloon. It'll be good to practice juggling." I called after him.

I tossed the balloon in the air and watched it land limply atop my IV stand. I shall try again when I inflate it.

A plethora of family, friends, nurses, orderlies and interns stopped in to comfort and/or examine me. Doc T popped in everyday just to chat about the 84% of my remaining lungs, minus the errant slice.

So far, so good. Only two things left on this leg of my to-do list: check the pathology report and check out. Let the healing begin. But, if everything was on course, how come there are so many pages left to this book. My curiosity had been piqued.

The Doc entered with the pathology report.

"Why so glum?" Doc T inquired.

"I can't juggle."

"Of course you can't," the Doc replied, "Maybe when the IV is removed."

"Well, Jan juggled right away — three balls — and didn't drop any behind the sofa."

"Jan? Did he have brain surgery? Juggling is a known side effect of brain surgery. Thirty six percent of all jugglers had prior brain surgery."

"Really?"

"No. I just made that up."

"Oh."

"It's really nineteen percent but nineteen percent didn't seem outstanding enough."

I hit the morphine again.

"Ok, I made that up too." Doc T checked my chart. "How are you feeling today?"

"Me? Couldn't be better. Feel great. We beat the parasitic bastard that squatted in my chest — slayed by your mighty sword or whatever you used."

"Robotic laser scalpel."

"Light saber." I waved my arm in a graceful swordsman-like tangling my IV tubes with the balloon string. Still, my recent conquest ruled my emotions.

Doc noticed my limp balloon hanging from the IV stand. "I don't believe that I prescribed that."

"I was practicing juggling."

He recovered it.

"It will probably work better when it's inflated." He observed.

"Yes."

"*Happy Bat Mitzvah?*" He read. "They must have been out of *Happy Lobectomy*. We've had quite a run on those — one of our most popular surgical-occasions. I'm waiting for them to get the *Happy Lobectomy* T-shirts with a big arrow pointing at the missing lobe. Good promo item. May put them on my website. How's the chest?"

"Good."

"Excellent."

"You were right. I don't miss the slice at all. In fact, I didn't even know it was gone except for the tubes hanging out of every part of my body, the IV and the backless hospital gown. Of course, the missing slice may inhibit my chances of running a marathon, which, if I ever get the opportunity, I wouldn't do anyway. But just saying. As soon as I am up to it, I shall begin to train to watch it on television."

The Doc overlooked my attempt at levity and issued a well-mannered bedside laugh.

"You know I was awake for most of the surgery." I mentioned as I untangled the balloon string only to wrap it around the TV remote. "Yep, didn't want to disturb you. You were kinda busy."

The Doc issued a wider, though less genuine, smile. Something was amiss. Not his joyous upbeat self, the Doc looked me in my serious eye and asked:

"Do you have an Oncologist?"

FUCK!

For the first time, I was afraid.

10

Go to the Bank,

Pick up the Cleaning,

Get Chemo

"Good morning, Richard." The strange voice on my voicemail blared through my phone. I knew that I didn't know her because I don't know that many recordings. She went on: "This is a reminder that you have chemotherapy on Friday when we will attempt to disintegrate and kill every toxic cell in your body. Of course, we may also annihilate many civilian women and children cells in the process. Please be appropriately anxious and concerned as we stick an intravenous in your arm and pump your body full of cancer poison. Have a wonderful day. Press one to listen again in Spanish, press two to repeat this menu, press three to hang up, or just hang up."

Ok. It wasn't quite like that but one cannot get into a chemo narrative positively. The pathology report showed one tiny, miniscule, infinitesimal, teeny weeny, little bit of cancer about one millimeter in diameter, hiding in a cardboard box in a lymph node close to the carcinoma. Technically, this reclassified my situation as Stage II, indicating that the cancer had spread beyond the carcinoma. It had been the earliest Stage II that Doc T had ever seen. The cute little bugger did not show up on X-rays, Catscans or Petscans. Only the biopsy revealed it. I was one-millimeter away from being cancer free.

Stage fuckin' II.

Eight weeks had passed since I celebrated the discovery and eradication of Stage I cancer and it turned out to be Stage II after all. I was pissed — not only did I have to go through chemo but my chances of survival had plummeted from a robust 49% to a mere 26%. From 50 – 50, even money, to three to one, against. Only one out of four make it. I did not want to be among the other three.

My invulnerability had been dinged once more. I picked it off the floor and folded it neatly and put it in my underwear drawer next to my favorite pair of briefs and my "Blackboard Monitor of the Year" trophy, which was a blackboard eraser with a post-it note stuck onto it.

My sentence was four treatments about three weeks apart. In about three months, this would be behind me. No matter how bad the process was, it was finite, like me. In the scheme of chemos, I guess that had been a pretty light stretch but it certainly didn't feel that way. Interestingly, I was far more apprehensive about chemotherapy than about surgery. Surgery had been cut and dry, except for the blood. I went to sleep and woke up with something missing; hopefully, it was all the bad stuff. Morph and I handled the pain quite adeptly and, each day, I looked forward to being better than the day before.

Chemo, however, promised to be a long engagement that would dominate my existence for the duration. The potential side effects bred apprehension, which bred tension and nervousness. I was ready. No I wasn't. But I was. Almost. But not really.

Ok, I dreaded it.

Even the best-case scenario seemed crummy. I decided to manage my expectations and turned instead to anticipating a bumpy, uncomfortable and vile journey. I put my optimism aside until the end of this leg of the journey, knowing that, on the other side of the chemo tunnel, was no chemo.

I had no doubts about the outcome.

Doc O's nurse entered.

"In the last three days," she asked, "Have you changed your meds or vitamins; . . ."

"No."

" . . . Moved to a different state or country; . . ."

"Uh uh."

" . . . Changed your insurance company, phone number; social security number; . . ."

"Nope."

" . . . Been abroad; kissed or licked anyone with smallpox, chicken pox or any of the known poxes; . . . "

"Nada."

" . . . Been deported; changed your birthday?"

"Negatory."

"Doc will be right with." She departed.

Doc O, an affable, oncological-looking man, sat on a stool across from me. He studied me as I did him.

"Don't believe everything you read or hear." He said.

I wondered if he knew that meant him as well. Of course, he said 'don't believe everything' which meant I could believe some things, unless what he said was part of the everything that I should not believe in which case I shall believe everything.

"Do you have any questions?" The affable Doc O inquired.

"Questions? Let me think." I thought. *Will the chemo fix everything? Will I lose my hair? Will it screw up my brain? How about my wry but acutely witty sense of humor? Can I have visitors? How long will it take? Will I get acne? Seriously, will I lose my hair? Will I be able to juggle afterwards? If I lose my hair, will I lose my eyebrows also? Not that I pay attention to them. I will try to be more attentive to my eyebrows in the future. Can I eat during chemo? Why me?* "Yes. Can I bring my IPad?"

"Certainly," Doc O chuckled. "Allow me to give you some do's and don'ts to make your chemo experience most enjoyable." He pulled out a long paper from the pocket of his white smock. He cleared his throat and read. "Don't go near babies, people with colds, people without colds, crowds, cattle, rallies, mobs, raves, riots, rebellions, particularly of Third or Fourth World countries. Let's see, people with rashes, sporting events with more than two people, outbreaks, plagues, scourges, epidemics, pandemics, or any of the known demics. Stay out of the sun but not too long but don't stay in the sun too long either. Also, don't watch TV shows or movies about any of the previous or hospital or doctor shows except those with Oncologist superheroes."

"What about the do's?"

"The do's?"

"Yes. You said do's and don'ts. You just gave me the don'ts. What about the do's?"

"Oh yes. Take it easy. Take a walk. Luxuriate. That's a do. You really have no choice because you won't feel like DO-ing anything." He raised an eyebrow to ensure that I received the pun in good order. He went on. "There really are no do's. I just said that to keep it balanced. You know, like *good news and bad news*, except there really isn't any good news except that there is no bad news either."

"Side effects?" I inquired.

"Ah yes. I almost forgot. Don't believe everything you read."

"Yes. You said."

"Chemo affects everyone differently. Did I say that?"

"No."

"Ok. Chemo affects everyone differently. Except, of course, Barney Friswall."

"Who?" I queried.

"Barney Friswall, not his real name of course." Doc O lowered his voice to a whisper. "Doctor/patient confidentiality. Chemo didn't affect him differently."

"Huh?"

"It affected him the same as everyone else. Only patient I've ever come across. Where was I? Oh yes. Side effects, which may or may not affect you, include: nausea, vomiting, leukemia, anorexia, diarrhea, weight loss, anemia, fever, neuropathy, tingling, numbness, loss of taste, blurred vision, wheezing, hair loss, fingernail ridges, dry mouth and/or skin, dark urine, low white blood cell count, risk of bleeding, fatigue, tiredness, listlessness, loss of appetite, constipation, mouth sores, rashes, tongue swelling, memory loss, infection and diarrhea."

"You said diarrhea twice."

"I did? I do that sometimes. Forget the second one. Let's see, what did I forget?" He took out his business card and flipped it over. "They're listed on the back."

"What are?"

"The side effects of chemo. Listed on the back." He continued perusing the back of his business card.

"Constipation?" I suggested.

"No, I think I said constipation. Constipation is one of my most popular side effects. No. Something like it."

"Infection?"

"Nope. I said infection. I always say infection. Dehydration! That's it. Dehydration." He smiled victoriously and spun a three sixty in his chair and slowed to a stop directly in front of me. We sat face to face.

"Here." The Doc handed me the business card. "They're listed on the back. Just in case. Great conversation starter for parties or in case Jeopardy comes up with a chemo category; never can tell. My name and phone are on the front. Website and email also. Don't forget to like me on Facebook."

Following the Doc's guidance, I read as much as I could and tried not to believe eighty percent of it. The twenty percent still sucked. Even though Doc O had said that chemo affects everyone differently, the options were still glum.

Down one lobe since the surgery, I remained perky and cautiously optimistic with a touch of hopeful apprehension and anxious trepidation. Not only was I concerned about whether the treatment would be ultimately successful in eradicating the aliens and saving the planet and all mankind but also I was apprehensive about the impact of the treatment itself. I readied for my first session. I had my iPad, my computer, a bottle of water, a magazine, a book that I would not read, and a roll of mints. The hospital would supply the TV, the IV and the assorted poisons.

A team of genial and skilled nurses attended and carefully explained the process. They would stick an IV into my arm and periodically change the secret sauce from hydration fluid to hemlock, or some such cancer-killing poison. Other than the initial pinch, the treatment had been without pain.

About half way through my first day, Nurse C approached, my chart tenderly cradled in her arm.

"Are you ready or do you need more time?" She inquired.

"More time?"

"To decide what side effects you're having."

"Almost forgot." I pulled Doc O's card from my pocket and perused the side effects menu carefully. It read like Marquis De Sade's lunch menu. "So many choices."

"Yes. We are all about the patient experience." She smiled.

"I'm ready." *I wasn't.*

"Ok. Shoot." Nurse C patiently stood over me with a pencil poised.

"I'll have . . ." I stalled momentarily. "Narrowing it down a bit. Ok. Got it." I looked up at her.

"Yes?" She stood unwearyingly.

"To start, I'll have slight weight loss, but only in the midsection area where I seemed to have put on a few extra pounds and . . . let's see . . . a side of occasional diarrhea, to assist in the weight loss. Is the diarrhea good here?"

"One of our most popular side effects. But if I may . . .?"

"Yes?"

"I would suggest some constipation to complement the diarrhea." Clearly, she understood her patients' palettes.

"Good idea. I'll have the constipation as well. But bring the constipation first."

"Of course." She wrote furiously. "That's it?"

"Not enough?"

"Most patients pick at least four side effects for the full chemo experience. After all, it's all included."

"I see." I picked up Doc O's card again. "Let's see. Oh yes. Can I get some hair loss?"

"We got some fresh this morning. You know, no one asks for that anymore."

"But can I lose it only in my armpits and behind my knees?"

"Shouldn't be a problem. I'll check with the doc. Eyebrows as well?"

"Skip the eyebrows. I think that's enough for starters."

"That it? Something for dessert? How about some fresh listlessness with a hint of half baked fatigue?"

I nodded negatively.

"A small rash or perhaps an irritating mouth sore?"

"I'm good."

Throughout the day, I peed frequently, measuring my output to ensure that I had adequately eliminated the toxins. I had a personal competition with myself to exceed the prior quantity, setting both personal best and hospital records. To honor my achievement, the nurses awarded me a certificate for *best first day yield* and hung it on the medicine refrigerator with a little magnet in the shape of a urinal.

I missed my catheter.

The chemo took eight, not unpleasant, hours. I felt fine when I left. The next day had been another matter.

11

Chemo is like Stubbing your Toe, Except it is Your Brain

Food tasted like Passover dinners at Aunt Selma's.

Tastes ranged from bland to flavorless with a slight hint of metallic au jus. Suddenly, meat tasted like old cardboard, bananas tasted like chalk and fruit tasted like my grandmother's old clothesline. Salt became the only flavor that would penetrate the pall.

Eating had become a matter of necessity. I needed to eat. I wanted to eat, but the pleasure of eating was a distant memory. Nevertheless, I consumed vast amounts of food, which created another problem.

Constipation produced tie-ups on all the major expressways as rush hour slowed to a crawl. The Alimentary Canal was backed up to the Esophagus Onramp causing a major pileup way downstream at the Duodenum Bypass. Indigestion sought alternate paths and found none — sending exhaust fumes into the atmosphere, felling pedestrians. Heartburn raged as rubberneckers slowed traffic to a complete standstill. My engine stalled and I overheated into cold sweats.

My system had entered complete gridlock. If I didn't go pretty soon, I wouldn't have room to swallow. I popped stool softeners like they were jellybeans as they slowly trudged their way through the massive obstruction. I awaited relief. I will never malign diarrhea again.

Around the third or fourth day following chemo, my energy level crashed. I sat, somewhere between nauseous and woozy, and I realized that queasy was my new normal. I wanted to leave my body and return when it got better. I didn't even have the power to deny my new reality. If I had the strength to walk, I could be a zombie, a minority with whom I began to empathize. I have never heard of a zombie being constipated or queasy from eating brains or noshing on flesh.

I shall not look down on the undead again.

I bottomed about ten days later and I realized that each cycle would repeat the pattern – about ten days of hell, ten days of slow restoration. Then, back to hell again. I tried to shape my daily plans around the cycle. However, each cycle became worse than the prior — the effect of chemo on chemo had been cumulative. I looked forward to worse before better, then even more worse and less better, and then ultimate worse and marginally better, followed by really shitty and, finally, a slow grueling ascent towards ok.

Passover dinner every night took its toll, as everything had the pungency of plain flavorless matzo without the ketchup or the matzo. Friends recommended healthy recipes like chemo soup, ingredients unknown. For all I know it could have been boiled zombie brains and kale. I did perceive a little flavor through the sole taste bud that survived the chemo offensive. Truthfully, the chemo soup brought some relief to my queasy. Whether that was a physiological breakthrough or just another delusion, did not matter. I believe that a properly induced perception is worth a dozen realities. So I had chemo soup and perceived the dis-queasing of my body.

Other things brought temporary relief — ginger chewies, green tea, antioxidants, protein/nutrient shakes, gargling with salt water, fiber, probiotics and a variety of chemo-fighting superhero drugs. I alternated between Imodium and stool softener with a ginger and fiber sandwich, followed by a refreshing salt-water gargle.

If I were big Pharma, I would invent a chemo poison that tasted like peppermint or maybe strawberry or Cheerios or sushi or steak or spaghetti. In fact, I would have a complete line of appetizing flavors for the chemo toxin, cleverly packaged in eye-catching juice boxes with colorful zombies on the front. Underneath the zombie picture would be:

> *ChemoAde*
> *Tastier than Brains*
> *(Only for the not undead yet)*

Of course, it would be carbonated so you could feel the *ChemoAde* tingle throughout your body whilst it hammered those invasive cancer cells into oblivion. A series of après-chemo salt mints, salt licorice, salty condiments and salt ice cream would complete my post-chemo food and nosh offering.

> *Après-Chemo Noshes*
> *For your last surviving taste bud*
> *(For the still living)*

My brain had paralleled my body into a state of mush. I had the mental acuity of a bowl of Wheatena. I had prided myself on my ability to effectively multi-process; now I could not string two thoughts together without losing focus. I could complete one thought if I could remember what it was.

Memory crashed as well – often forgetting what I forgot. Heretofore priding myself on great recall, now I found it flawed, sometimes inoperative. It seemed that I could store things but just couldn't recall them. They were in there somewhere or maybe they weren't. I just had to plod through the closets of my mind and keep throwing out crap until I found what I had been looking for. Of course, sometimes, I would forget what I was looking to remember, forgetting what I forgot, which chemo whizzes dubbed a *double forget*. I am surprised that I remembered the forgetting of what I forgot to write about it.

A computer virus hacked my head – nothing functioned properly. My peripherals froze and my RAM was unresponsive. My GUI was gooey. I rebooted frequently but Windows froze at startup. I took extreme measures and had Norton scan my brain and sweep all errant cookies and unapproved apps. MacAfee jumped in and killed all unauthorized pop-ups and spam. Hoping to improve responsiveness, I defragged my memory and drives and backed everything up to the cloud which was where I was most of the time. Communication was askew. I considered switching out my medulla for a Mac.

I tried brain exercises and signed up for an online brain/memory game/exercise until I forgot to do them. I think that's what bothered me the most, losing my acuity, my sharpness, my quick-witted repartee and something else, which eludes me. I plodded through the mental morass, knowing at the end of the tunnel, I would be somewhat restored to my former position of acutely clever and sharp with a touch of snarky wit.

Or would I? Maybe this would be the new me.

Jan, my bro-in-law-in-law, visited. We now had another bond as mutual wannabe cancer survivors. Again I was reminded that as bad as I felt with the hardship of chemo, his situation had been more dire. He had brain surgery. Yet, he visited me. Nice.

He brought another chemo combatant in the form of a chocolate chip marijuana cookie and a joint. I hesitated — it had been many years since I partook in the euphoria and elation of the chocolate chip. My brain had been operating on one faulty cylinder. I didn't want to lose whatever clarity remained so I put both in the freezer for a celebratory occasion. Besides, the cookie would have tasted like cardboard. Perhaps I would not have cared.

Doc O had said that chemo affects everyone differently. I anticipated and readied for the most popular chemo effect: hair loss, an art I had been practicing over the years. I made up my mind that if my hair is going, I am going to be the one who did it. So I cut it short, real short. I wrested a moment of control from a previously uncontrollable situation and did it to myself before it was done to me. The way I look at it, it's only hair, so what.

Each morning I checked the pillow for a hair count. I gently picked up each errant hair and laid it in a place of final rest. I recorded the event on my *hair loss rate spreadsheet* that I had created years earlier in VisiCalc upon detecting my first hair in the sink. After having long hair my whole life, short hair had been unthinkable. Sometimes we need an external stimulus to perceive things differently.

Time to change.

12

Bonjour Broccoli,
Au Revoir French Fries

I made up my mind; I was not going to be like Barney Friswall. I wasn't going to be the same; I would be different just like everyone else.

Even if the chemo worked, the cancer could return. Perhaps the chemo doesn't wipe out the cancer population as we had hoped. What if a tiny one-millimeter cancer cell was asleep in a lymph node in my pinky toe? I was pretty sure that Catscans don't cover pinky toes. And even if the chemo worked, what if I just get cancer again, the same way I got it this time, whatever that was?

I had to do something different.

I resisted cutting my hair shorter for years. Now, an external event caused me to do it and I feel pretty good about it. I guess we all get caught in our safe groove, our cozy track of life where change is unthinkable until it is absolutely necessary. Sometimes we need a detour from a familiar route we've travelled for many years. Suddenly, we are forced into a new arena, a new venue and a new path — maybe better, certainly different.

My proverbial wind had shifted. I straddled the brink of the watershed of an inflection point in my life. This moment would serve as a point of demarcation that separated the old from the new, the past from the future, and the *was* from the *will be*. This would be a defining moment, much like the moment that I gave up blackboard monitoring as a potential vocation. My parents had been disappointed but I had to look at the long haul and forgo the recognition and status that certainly would accompany professional blackboard monitoring. Family traditions die hard; my parents' legacy had been stopped cold. But such is the way of change.

Yes, I would make a left turn from the right lane of my life. The cancer had awakened the sleeping giant.

No more Mr. Sometimes-Pretty-Nice Guy. *This was war!* I had to build up my body to wage an internal war 24/7.

I launched a three-pronged attack:

1. Eat right
2. Exercise
3. Try not to fall asleep during dinner

I had checked with Doc O and he said that diet was not a significant issue, "no more that it would be if you were cancer-free." The nurses said; "Moderation. I should follow a healthy diet but an occasional break or treat would be ok." Google had a plethora of information to sift through it all and come up with my own diet.

I knew that I couldn't do this alone. I had to get guidance and support. I needed a trusted advisor — someone with expertise and fortitude and patience.

"Sugar kills." Hochman muttered as he sipped a cup of decaf in my kitchen as I drooled into my green tea.

I nodded as I propped my head on my hand, carefully locking my elbow in place so it wouldn't slip like yesterday when I plunged face first into a bowl of Wheatena loaded with sugar and butter.

"And butter kills."

I nodded again.

"Ok, if you are serious, you have to change some things and when I say some things, I really mean everything. You in?"

I nodded or maybe I didn't. I can't quite remember. I lost track of my nodding. I sipped some green tea to load up on antioxidants and to keep my elbow from getting numb.

"Broccoli." Hochman declared as if he had just planted his flag on the moon.

"Broccoli?" I managed to repeat quizzically.

"Broccoli, the archenemy of chemotherapy and cancer. Makes your body strong twelve ways. Look it up."

"Asking you is like looking it up. You are my own personal Google. You should get a Hochman logo."

"Are you going to do this?"

"Yep. Broccoli. The kryptonite of chemo."

"And cancer."

"And cancer. What else?"

"Load up on antioxidants, protein, leafy greens, the deeper the color the better." Hochman waited while I wrote. "And . . ."

I wrote slowly as I leaned onto my pen for support. I may have fallen asleep for a tad.

"Hydrate, kale, green tea, fish, but no crustaceans." He continued patiently. "And no sugar; sugar energizes the rat bastard cancer cells. Rat bastards. Sugar kills."

"Rat bastard sugar." I echoed to assure him that I had been, in fact, listening. "Bastards."

"And lighten up on dairy. No cheese." He went on.

"I can't cut out cheese."

"You think you can't, but you can. You are the new you or you will be once you change. Think positive. Think different. Think new you. Think new new you." Saliva started to build on his lower lip forming a small bubble. "The old you has left the room, the new you has just walked in arm in arm with yourself. Everyone turns and says 'who is that guy?' And you, the new you, walks into the room on a cloud of confidence and say: 'hi, this is the new me.'"

Hochman looked at me for a reaction to his vision.

"Yes," I said, without knowing quite what I said yes to.

"Everything is in play." He stood and the bubble morphed into a small drool. He pointed skyward as his arm entangled with the venetian blinds. "This is your tabula rasa, your fresh start. Sacrifice." The drool turned into spittle and dispersed into the atmosphere. "You," he pointed at me through the venetian blinds. "You, the new you, can cut out cheese."

He sat.

"No, I really can't cut it out."

"You can."

"No, I really can't because I don't eat it, particularly American cheese. I don't eat American cheese more than I don't eat all other cheeses combined except maybe Gorgonzola, which I will never try mostly because of the name. If it was called french fries cheese or cherry vanilla cheese, I may try it, but probably not. Don't even like mac and cheese or, forgive me, Cheez Wiz." I stirred my tea and lost my breath. I brought my cup to my mouth to buy time. The spoon wedged into my eye. I left it there.

Hochman stared in disbelief as he finally disentangled himself.

I removed the spoon from my eye and stared back at him. Clearly he had been disappointed at my rejection of his very first recommendation as my mentor. I had to offer something to show that I was playing ball, some token to cross the line into the new and improved moi.

"I know," I offered, "how about Cheese Doodles? I can cut them out. Done. I have begun the change."

Hochman remained unimpressed.

"And no red meat." He went on. "If you do, make it organic, grass fed. Eat fish, chicken, turkey, pheasant but no processed meat."

"Processed meat?"

"Salami, Bacon, Prosciutto, Sausage, pastrami ..."

"No bacon?"

"No bacon."

"No processed meat and eggs?"

"Nope."

"No PMLT?"

"Nope."

"Jeez."

I had spent sixty plus years cultivating finely tuned bad habits to perfection. I would have to kiss them goodbye. I made a list of my favorite foods and put an X through it. This was the end of an era.

I wrote a note.

Sweeties:

Goodbye my old friends. Goodbye red licorice, goodbye chocolate, goodbye soda with lunch and dinner. Adios mi tacos, hamburgers and hotdogs. Au revoir french fries. Ciao sausage, prosciutto, bacon and other heretofore unspecified processed meats.

Goodbye ice cream and occasional candy — I shall miss you Chuckles, Jujyfruits and Good & Plenty, you knuckleheads. You brought many smiles. And so long to you, Twizzlers, I have always appreciated your flexibility and elasticity.

And to my favorites: Hershey's, Nestlé's Crunch and especially M&Ms, with and without peanuts. Yes, M&Ms, I will miss you most of all except the blue M&Ms, which never really belonged — but I shall miss them as well. I shall forever believe that they should have had a separate package for blue M&Ms but it is not for me to decide any longer.

And to so many others with whom I have shared many sweet moments through the years. I shall miss you old friends. Be well.

Au Revoir Confectionaire

Cancer was a bitch. I think nature screwed up the grand design. In my scenario, cancer should feed on American cheese and falafel and perhaps asparagus. Conversely, chocolate, ice cream and bacon would be loaded with antioxidants and toxic proteins that were deadly to every cancer cell. Had my design been in play, cancer probably would not have attained the popularity that it had today. Imagine,

Glebe's Anti-Malignant Chocolate Chunk Ice Cream
Ice cream for the living

So I did it, little by little, eliminating the old and bringing in the new.

Chemo had made everything taste like shit so the transition had been much easier. Instead of going from something I liked to something I maybe could like but didn't yet, I went from shitty tasting to shitty tasting. Then I got used to the new shitty tasting which didn't taste so shitty because it, at least, tasted like something that wasn't metallic. Instead of going cold turkey, which would have been more challenging, the after effects of chemo allowed me to stage my withdrawal and go from established habits to neutral to new habits, with minimal discomfort. To summarize, I successfully wiped out my old eating memory and replaced it in part with a newer rebuilt model.

Each week I had a *sanctioned cheat day* where I could lightly splurge on ice cream or a small piece of chocolate to reward myself for being so controlled. In keeping with the spirit of the program, I opted for sugar-free ice cream and natural chocolate. Not only did I change my bodily intake, I felt emotionally worthy.

Perhaps some of my immaturity had finally dissipated.

Perhaps not.

13

Exercise was the Ticket -
So I Hired a Kid to Run for Me

I had one foot out of my safe groove.

Changing my eating habits was only part of the puzzle; I had to exercise. I hate exercise. Let me be clear; I enjoy playing ball, tennis, skiing, and so forth. I just don't like the loneliness, the repetitiveness, the boredom, and the routine of pure exercise. There are many who enjoy the rigor of a tough workout — a jog, a run, a pump of the iron, but I am not among them. I don't mind walking if I were going someplace or running to catch a fly ball but just to walk or run without an immediately gratifying reward at the tail end bored me. Treadmills were for hamsters, not people.

I had always been envious of people who exercised and enjoyed it. Their endorphins experienced an exhilaration that mine could never attain. My endorphins just stayed home enjoying a game of video Pong or watching a football game to experience a taste of what could be. Alas, my endorphins had been underprivileged and underutilized.

I did admit that exercise was necessary for good health, a strong body and a strong mind, particularly in my situation. I finished my last chemo and my strength should gradually return. But I had to strengthen my core so my body could fight any future battles with cancer should they arise. I needed to exercise; I wanted to exercise. No, I didn't. Ok, I did . . . but I really didn't. But I knew that it was good for me, so I did.

I really didn't.

Confronted with a conundrum of sorts, I, once again, rose to the occasion, meeting the challenge of the conundrum head on. I had a solution. Not the kind of solution that one finds within the box — a more creative, innovative, and heretofore, unthought of and unused solution— a simple, yet elegant, solution to a perturbing problem that required urgent attention and resolution.

I hired a kid to run for me.

I had him start slowly. After all, I am still recovering from three months of chemo — a mile a day for starters. For a frail kid, he did pretty well. But between his frailty and my post chemo reclamation, I knew I could not have him overdo it. Then, the second week, as the distance from my last chemo widened, I moved him up to two miles. He strained at first, but he did it. Then, three miles a day. I would like to point out that these were not three flat miles on a smooth road on sunny yet cool days. He ran an uphill route of irregular terrain, in both clement and inclement weather.

Then, three point two miles.

Yes, I know what you are probably thinking:

Are you crazy? Three point two miles in just the third week? Uphill? In clement and inclement weather?

Yes, I pushed it. I had been determined to beat this thing.

By the time I awoke each morning, the kid had finished running, overcast or shine. But strangely, after three solid weeks of grueling training, I felt little difference in my bod. I wondered where my endorphins had been hiding — perhaps extricated with my upper right lobe and the pepperoni? It wasn't working. Three weeks of the kid's intensive training and yet I still sludged out of bed, crawled to the bathroom to brush my own teeth and count the hair in my sink.

Again, I know what you are thinking:

Jeez. It's only been three weeks. Give it some time. You just came out of chemo, you know.

Perhaps. But I had a goal in mind and conventional wisdom would not work for me. Maybe you were correct and three weeks had not been enough time to reap the benefits of my innovative exercise program but patience had never been an asset of the successful cancer killer. I persevered.

I pressed to three and a half miles. Yet my expectation of renewed vigor had not been achieved. Disappointed but not defeated, I pushed onward. I pressed the kid to four miles.

But something was amiss — I still felt tired and weak and fatigued with a touch of listlessness and lethargy. I had planned this effort with much thought and care — perhaps it was the execution. I had to find out. So one slightly overcast morn with a threat of intermittent showers, I followed the kid on his daily route. Alas, I discovered the problem. The kid left my house, turned the corner and hung with his friends for an hour. No wonder I had not felt the surge of vitality through my body.

I fired the kid.

Hiring a kid to run for me was a really inane idea. In fact, it was very dumb. I am quite ashamed at my lack of thoughtlessness and due diligence. I could have blamed it on the chemo-induced-bread-pudding state of mind but I take full responsibility for a dumb plan and even dumber execution. Hiring a kid had absolutely no chance of working — I should have hired an older, more responsible, adult to run for me.

And I did.

Alas, after interviewing several candidates I hired an older, more responsible, adult. It paid off big time. In week four, a watershed event.

I popped out of bed; my endorphins partied, my electrolytes scurried throughout my body and my adrenal glands spewed adrenalin. Renewed strength and vitality flowed through my legs and up into my thoracic cavity as the endorphins nudged my sleeping dopamine awake. My brain overflowed with synaptic glee. My body toned quickly and I had been filled with abundant energy.

I pushed the older, more responsible, adult to five miles. This had no end. I had always wanted to bulk up my upper body so I considered hiring another older, more responsible, adult to pump iron for me. I should have thought of this earlier and hired an older, more responsible, adult to go to the dentist for me and to get chemo for me . . .

Ok, I may have stretched the truth a tad. I am truly sorry for that and, if I could undo the previous paragraphs, I would.

I did exercise — stretches at first, then some light lifting of forks and knives, oft adding food for protein and nourishment. Then, some light weights to regain some muscle tone that I never had. For cardio, I took walks to nowhere and back and I bought a stationary bike so I could exercise in bed. I was on the road to recovery.

The chemo tunnel was behind me along with the surgery.

I had my first post-surgery and post-chemo Catscan coming up....

14

Was it all for Naught?

About six weeks after my last chemo treatment I began to feel almost normal –although I really forgot what that was. Each day had been a tad better than the day before except for last Tuesday when I missed recycling for the second time.

My next checkpoint was the big one, the one that would prove how successful the last few months had been. It was akin to a final exam, although, hopefully, not a final exam. More like a midterm — a giant midterm of life. This was *the* test — no grades, just pass or fail.

I thought of Jan. After his first brain surgery, he had another brain surgery — and after that, another surgery on his leg. Cancer was a resilient invasive bastard. Each time you get a small victory, the threat of another attack lay silently in the wings. There was no victory, no big win, just small battles that get you closer to procrastinating the return of the toxic avenger. The key is to delay it forever, as long as forever lasts a long time.

Jan was a fighter — I rooted for him. I couldn't help but to relate to my own situation, nowhere near as dire as Jan's, yet, my vulnerability surfaced. I took all steps to eradicate the terrorist cells, yet the remnants of worry tiptoed in.

Did everything work as planned/hoped? Were there a few errant microbes of cancer loitering in some alley in my chest or in my pinky toe or my ear lobe? Did the surgery work? Did the chemo work? Was my diet worth it? Was my worry for naught?

I lay there on the transport bed waiting to be teleported through the Catscan machine. I couldn't help recall that my last Catscan revealed my two and a half foot adenocarcinoma.

"Did you clean the machine?" I tactfully inquired of the technician. "I mean . . . to make sure that there are no splotches. Just saying."

"I check for splotches every morning." He said as he prepped me for an IV. "Last splotch I had on my Catscans was over ten years ago. And then it showed a real splotch in the patient's lungs — first one in this country. Imagine that, a splotch. Who knows what would have happened if we didn't catch it early — could've been a splotchdemic, spread worldwide? Anyway, we caught it in this very machine. They did a Splotchectomy, the first Splotchectomy in history. We still have one of the best Splotch Surgeons and Splotchectomy Departments in the country. Put this hospital on the map — it's in all of the brochures. By the way, the guy is still doing great. Sends me a Christmas card every year." I detected a tad of sarcasm.

"Don't forget the pinky toe." I reminded a little meekly.

"Got both of them covered. Along with your ear lobes." He assured as he slowly inserted the IV with contrast dye in my vein.

The IV pain shot through my arm. I camouflaged the hurt with a teeth-clenching yelp and a couple of tears followed by the tiniest of whimpers. I inquired about the possibility of acquiring a wooden stick to hold between my teeth.

Other than an uncomfortable IV insertion for the contrast dye, the Catscan was uneventful. The next step was to meet with Doc T in a few days to get the results.

My confidence in my delusional optimism was unwavering, until now. I lay in bed the night before and couldn't sleep. Not given to unnecessary worry, which was all worry as far as I was concerned, my worry worried me.

I kept thinking about that errant, teeny weeny, one millimeter, instance of cancer that squatted in one of my lymph nodes. If it was in that lymph node, it could be in other lymph nodes, many lymph nodes, maybe every lymph node. But, no one was certain that it had gone beyond the solitary node that had been removed along with the rest of the slice of pizza. Presumably, the chemo was preventative, a pre-emptive strike to destroy the little squatters cowering in my innocent lymph nodes, should they exist. And, if they do not exist, it would serve as a stern warning. But the way I looked at it, they existed. If the bugger was in one lymph node, they were in others. Napalm the bastards.

Had that tiny instance not been there, had I not been the earliest Stage II on record, had I not gotten cancer in the first place, there would have been no chemo reminder voicemail and no chemo. But there was. I would be more confident but every step of this journey had the promise of being the last step and turned out otherwise. What was a nagging cough turned to pneumonia which it wasn't, which turned into stage one cancer which it wasn't, which turned into stage two cancer. Was it? Hopefully, chemo was the last step. But was it?

If I had to choose, I think that I would rather have surgery than chemo. It was so much easier and I missed my old friends — Mr. Catheter and Mr. Morphine.

Admittedly, I was a tad anxious. I know; it was normal to be anxious in an anxiety filled emotional experience where the stakes were high. But I don't experience anxiety that often so it made me nervous.

The nurse checked my vitals prior to the Doc entering — they were all there. Doc T had reviewed my Catscan results before entering the exam room. I fully expected that he would pop in with a handful of confetti and say: "You passed! Have a good summer."

We waited.

What if the chemo didn't work? What next? Will I have to get chemo again? Surgery? Both? Radiation? Chemo-surgical-radiation therapy? Should I consider Eastern medicine, go holistic?

Doc T entered, affable, yet business-like and professional as always, confetti-free. He chitchatted about recent events, unrelated to the subject at hand, somewhat procrastinating the news that both Virginia and I wanted to hear. In fact, had this been my meeting, he could have stuck his hand in the door with a thumbs-up or thumbs-down sign. We discussed his recent vacation and his wedding anniversary, which, as it turned out, was on the same day as ours. Not only the same date but also the exact same day, thirty years earlier. Really. I wondered about other coincidences that we might have shared.

"Were you ever a blackboard monitor?" I inquired as he checked my vitals once again. I snuck a look into his pocket to see if he had confetti secreted there.

Doc T was a nice guy and an excellent surgeon so we gave him the courtesy of listening to his meanderings until he broke the news. Let me be clear — we had no problem with what he was saying or how he said it. We just wanted him to modify the order of his message. Let us know the *news* first, chit chat later.

We waited patiently, anxious as the tension accumulated within. Then, somewhere mid-sentence . . .

"By the way, your Catscan was clear," he finally uttered matter-of-factly, through a wry smile.

I suspected that he intentionally intensified the anticipation making the good news even more meaningful. He had built the expectation and introduced a tiny shred of doubt before breaking the good news. As long as the news was good, it was ok with me. He could savor it for as long as he liked before sharing it. Brilliant marketing.

I looked at Virginia and she at me, both of us restrained in our glee. We've been down this road before. In fact, every step of this journey had a U-turn at the end. We needed to do our due diligence before we would join in the celebration. I knew exactly what question to ask.

"Did you check my pinky toe?" I inquired into his stethoscope.

"Of course. Checked them first — and your ear lobes. Everything is clean."

I was satisfied.

We celebrated with two slices of pizza.

15

Dear Cancer,

Up Yours

One year into my cancer tunnel —since it was discovered and surgically eradicated: about eight months since I finished chemo. And now I have successfully passed my first and second Catscan checkpoints and feel pretty good about that. Most of the tunnels are in my rear view. With two Catscans down — twenty percent of the way there — and eight more to go in my five-year cancer-free quest.

I wondered about my odds of survival after the surgery and chemo and almost a year of being cancer-free. After checking Google and poring over several authoritative websites, I decided that the numbers were irrelevant. Those are history, other people's numbers, not my numbers. My future is not based on someone else's history; it's based on me, what I've done, what I do and who I am. Clearly, no one else has my history or my future. No one else has won the *P.S. 222 Blackboard Monitor of the Year* and had an almost near perfect attendance record. Certainly, no one else has been a doofus with a pipe on a bike.

The journey has had some good takeaways. I still maintained my new and improved diet, fortified by Virginia's cooking and Hochman's nudging. No more fries, bacon, M&Ms, et al. But I did open other doors and I found that I actually do like other things; broccoli wasn't so bad if I chewed and swallowed quickly and turkey bacon was an ok substitute. I've lightened up on carbs and stopped drinking soda.

I guess it took a potential life threatening disease to get me out of my safe groove and, truthfully, I am better for it. Somehow, I had been awakened to the possibility that I was not invulnerable. Maturity had crept in ever so lightly.

There had been many moments of temptation when I could have easily justified breaking my new credo, just once. I have occasionally wandered down the candy aisle at the local supermarket, just because I could. The sweet fragrance of the Hersey's Milk Chocolate, with and without almonds, penetrated my senses. In the background, I could hear the Good & Plenty giggling with the Chuckles, bidding me to join them. In one of my proudest moments, which I certainly shall tell to my grandchildren, and hopefully they will retell to their own children, I caressed a package of Twizzlers. Their suppleness and pliability had been a sensual temptation. I had been wooed into an unbreakable seductive embrace. In the past, a lesser me would have succumbed. I thought: *just this once.*

But I gently laid the package down in its rightful place on the shelf and walked away without looking back. I departed the supermarket, better for it, yet leaving a part of me behind.

Virginia tactfully reminded me that I had left the groceries behind so I returned to the supermarket shortly thereafter. To my surprise, I noticed several other orphaned carts sitting randomly in the candy aisle. I knew then that others survivors must be out there as well. I raised my eyes skyward into the glow of the fluorescent lights that hung far above the candy aisle and all of the other aisles that housed abandoned carts full of every food group, paper goods and assorted household cleaning items.

77

It's good to know that I was not alone in the journey. And I hoped that each survivor would return to find his or her cart safely intact. As an anonymous gesture of brotherhood and support, I adorned each forsaken cart with a flower of broccoli draped over a fresh salmon.

I realize how close I came — if not for a few good decisions and a lot of good fortune. Thanks to the female posse, the doctors, nurses, chemo nurses, friendly hospital receptionists and most of all Doc H and Virginia and my friends and my family who were incredibly supportive.

I have learned a bit along the way:

- Listen to the women in your life more often. From now on, I will pay a tad more attention — even more than I had in the past, which was considerable, except sometimes.
- Bring Windex to your Catscan.
- Keep whatever immaturity you can. I shall forever be the doofus on the bike.
- If you have a little cough take him to your doctor and do not put him under the bed in a shoebox because it's hard to breathe unless you punch little holes in it.
- Worry is very time consuming.
- Do not hire a kid to do exercise for you. Find a more responsible older adult.
- Get out of your safe groove, now. Do it. Go.
- Enjoy the bridges while you can.
- Endure the tunnels with optimism.
- Write a note just in case. Better yet, just tell people.
- Eat nutritiously. Do not try broccoli-flavored ice cream, even if it's sugar free.

- Pick your doctor carefully and ask questions particularly if he mentions pepperoni. Do not ask about frequent flyer points.
- Get a second opinion. You'll probably ignore it but at least you will feel better about your ultimate decision.
- Check Google to see if your doctor is right.
- Always remember to recycle.
- Be different; don't be like Barney Friswall.
- Chemo is like stubbing your toe, except it is your brain.
- I didn't like chemo that much but I was too tired to know the difference.
- During chemo, your IQ will plummet to that of a bowl of Wheatena.
- Breathing is good.
- Stay eternally optimistic; nothing else makes sense.
- Give up cheese; if you don't like cheese, try it and then give it up.
- If you have Chemo, it's best to alternate the diarrhea and constipation side effects.
- Shark proof your basement and it wouldn't hurt to add a *sharks in the basement* rider to your home insurance.
- M&Ms don't have many antioxidants
- Do not shower with two or more supermodels at the same time.
- Have a friend like Hochman to guide you when you don't want guidance and to put up with your crap in spite of not being related to you and you don't owe them money.
- Learn to juggle.
- There is not much call for Blackboard Monitors no matter how good you are.
- Splotches are not terminal to humans.

- Near-perfect attendance records are not regarded as highly as Perfect Attendance records because you are absent more.
- Know how to calculate percentages so you will understand your chances of survival and know which bills to pay.
- Survival percentages are not that important unless, of course, they are in your favor.
- Catheters are time saving and convenient as long as you're not going anywhere.
- Keep a list of people who you think would not go to your funeral and don't go to theirs if the occasion should arise.
- Do not be a pipe-smoking, bike-riding, doofus. You can be a doofus without the pipe.
- I have not seen any signs of sharks in my basement or front lawn. It figures, now that I have insurance, they don't show up.

The way I look at it, you can only control so much, usually not enough, certainly far less than we would like to. That's what makes it challenging. So you need some way to get from here to there, some way to ride the speed bumps and potholes. We coast through the bridges, the highs of life, where you glide along, enjoying the sunshine, hoping/thinking the bridge never ends.

Tunnels are the hard part. Cancer was one long tunnel; surgery and chemo were tunnels inside the cancer tunnel. Knowing that they would soon be in the distant past drove me forward. And, if by chance I was a tad incorrect and I didn't prevail, nothing was lost by feeling positive throughout. In fact, the journey had been far more tolerable, because I had been confident that I would be among the reigning 49% (or the more up to date, 26%). Whatever the number or the process, my goal had always been to wake up in the morning and look forward to the day. I see no reason to stop that now.

I think about Jan. We had become bonded in our parallel catastrophes. Since his initial surgery, which preceded mine by only a few weeks, his cancer had returned, requiring a second surgery. The little bastards showed up in other parts of his body as well. But Jan has a strong will and body and he is a fighter. I chalk my journey up to an unpleasant, yet educational, experience. A lesson learned. Jan's journey was significantly more rugged and treacherous.

I'm pretty sure I'll make it. I'm pulling for Jan.

Keep juggling Jan.

Appendix: The Note 1.0

The following Note is still valid unless Note 2.0 has been released. Please check your latest downloads.

* * *

Just in Case

(**This Note was written pre-surgery**)

Hi everybody

I thought about writing something just in case ... even though I really believe that there will be no '*just in case*'. So if you are reading this, I was wrong, unless you are scouring through my desk for a pen, a rubber band or some loose change.

I love you. You are truly great people and a greater family.

I love you Virginia. Thank you for your grace and love and being by my side through many ups and occasional downs. We have always managed to understand each other-back off when it was called for, support when support was needed, and sometimes ignore each other's shortcomings. You are a great partner and a great friend. I have truly appreciated our life together and, if I had to do over, would not change a thing.

I love you Mom. Thank you for the unconditional love and support from before I even knew about it. You nurtured my talents, gave me the values I have and made me who I am. I could not conceive of a better and more loving mother. You seemed to always know what was going on inside and dealt with the issues that needed dealing with and overlooked those that best be passed.

I love you Scott and Christy. Thank you for being the greatest son and daughter and people I could ever imagine. You are truly unique, loving and special. I am so glad you're born. Both of you have made me especially proud of who you are, how you deal with life, your sensitivity, your devotion to the family, the children you have and will have and for the incredibly wonderful mates you have both picked. With each of you I have shared a very unique bond that I can't imagine exists elsewhere.

I love you Kim and Michael. Thank you for being you. I think that you are each a special fit for your partner. Each of you has made the family more wholesome, more loving and more fun.

I love you Parker and T.J. and Pebbles. Thank you for being fun and loving and nice to each other. I am very proud of you. You make me very very happy.

I love you Jicki Jacki thank you for being my foil sometimes, my partner always – I think that I enjoyed being on your Shitlist as much a being on your Christmas list. I appreciate your unwavering support and care. I enjoyed playing with you, picking on you (with love) and being your brother and friend.

I love you Don – thank you for sometimes being my younger brother and sometimes being the older brother. I love the way our relationship has grown over the years — Pop would have been proud — he always told us not to play on opposite teams.

I love you Larry – thank you for being a great bro-in-law. Your support and caring and love have always been appreciated. I love you Barb –thank you for the warmth, the light, the spirit, and the will.

I love you Carrie and Aaron – and the nest you have built.

I love you Ziggy, Brandi and Raven. Be good to Mommy and behave yourselves.

I love you my good friends, Ritchie, Michael and Hugh and to the many old and new friends that have been caring and supportive throughout. Thank you for being good friends longer than forever.

And Dawn, and Aunt Selma and Uncle Irving and so many others.

If I did not mention you specifically, rest assured that you are on the bubble of my thoughts. I could go on and on thanking and appreciating all of the special relationships I've had with so many people. If I did, this list and this note would never end.

Be happy, miss me a little, but never lose your sense of family or your sense of humor.

me

Ritch Gaiti is an author, an artist and a former Wall Street Executive. He focuses on telling compelling stories within a wide range of subjects and genres: from drama to suspense to humor, from fiction to non-fiction.
Ritch's published works include:

- THE JEWOLIC (Sedona Editions, 2013), Conundrums of a Half-Jew – a humorous romp through religious ambivalence.
- THE BIG EMPTY, (Sedona Editions, 2013), an ethereal mystery about a gritty lawyer who uncovers an ancient conspiracy.
- DUTCHING THE BOOK (Sedona Editions, 2012), a fictional drama based on real people and events, delivers an absorbing story about horse racing and gambling in 1960's Brooklyn.
- TWEET, a fictional satire on marketing, advertising and consumerism. TWEET has been optioned for a feature film.
- POINTS: WOMEN HAVE THEM, MEN NEED THEM, a humorous relationship book which will help you through this marriages and all your future marriages (written under the pseudonym I. Glebe).

All books can be found on www.RitchGaiti.com.

Ritch has also written articles for magazines, including Private Wealth, Sidelines, Tango and Balance magazines and has been featured on national TV and radio, including a guest appearance on the Today Show, opposite Joan Rivers.
In addition to writing, Ritch is a recognized artist who exhibits regularly in galleries and museums across the

country. His portfolio can be viewed on: www.Gaiti.com. He is also a recreational pilot and enjoys tennis and skiing.

To contact Ritch directly: Ritch.Gaiti@verizon.net

Made in the USA
Monee, IL
09 April 2020

25453847R00051